Revelation

'Christian believers have always found the opening chapters of Revelation a wonderful source of devotional encouragement. These notes from Paul Mallard provide a brilliantly accessible resource that will profit believers at any stage of their Christian lives.'
Steve Midgley, Senior Minister, Christ Church, Cambridge, and Executive Director, Biblical Counselling UK

'What rich food indeed is served up with these terrific short devotionals from the Letters to the Seven Churches. Paul Mallard does three things so very well: he opens up the text faithfully, he connects to people warmly and, above all, he lifts up Jesus in all his magnificence. Readers are in for a real treat – and, if taken to heart, this book will do you the power of good. Warmly commended.'
Ray Evans, pastor, Grace Community Church, Bedford, and Church Leadership Consultant, Fellowship of Independent Evangelical Churches

30-DAY DEVOTIONAL

Revelation

Paul Mallard

with Elizabeth McQuoid

FOOD
FOR THE
JOURNEY

INTER-VARSITY PRESS
36 Causton Street, London SW1P 4ST, England
Email: ivp@ivpbooks.com
Website: www.ivpbooks.com

First published 2018

British Library Cataloguing-in-Publication Data
A catalogue record for this book is available from the British Library.

ISBN: 978–1–78359–712–3
eBook ISBN: 978–1–78359–713–0

Typeset in Great Britain by CRB Associates, Potterhanworth, Lincolnshire
Printed in Great Britain by Ashford Colour Press Ltd, Gosport, Hampshire

Inter-Varsity Press publishes Christian books that are true to the Bible and that communicate the gospel, develop discipleship and strengthen the church for its mission in the world.

IVP originated within the Inter-Varsity Fellowship, now the Universities and Colleges Christian Fellowship, a student movement connecting Christian Unions in universities and colleges throughout Great Britain, and a member movement of the International Fellowship of Evangelical Students. Website: www.uccf.org.uk. That historic association is maintained, and all senior IVP staff and committee members subscribe to the UCCF Basis of Faith.

Preface

Can you guess how many sermons have been preached from the Keswick platform? Almost 6,500!

For over 140 years, the Keswick Convention in the English Lake District has welcomed gifted expositors from all over the world. The convention's archive is a treasure trove of sermons preached on every book of the Bible.

This series is an invitation to mine that treasure. It takes talks from the Bible Reading series given by well-loved Keswick speakers, past and present, and reformats them into daily devotionals. Where necessary, the language has been updated but, on the whole, it is the message you would have heard had you been listening in the tent on Skiddaw Street. Each day of the devotional ends with a newly written section designed to help you apply God's Word to your own life and situation.

Whether you are a convention regular or have never been to Keswick, this Food for the Journey series is a unique opportunity to study the Scriptures with a Bible teacher by your side. Each book is designed to fit in your jacket pocket or handbag so you can read it anywhere – over the breakfast table, on the commute into work or college, while you are waiting in your car, over your lunch break or in bed at night. Wherever life's journey takes you, time in God's Word is vital nourishment for your spiritual journey.

Our prayer is that these devotionals become your daily feast, a precious opportunity to meet with God through his Word. Read, meditate, apply and pray through the Scriptures given for each day, and allow God's truths to take root and transform your life.

If these devotionals whet your appetite for more, there is a 'For further study' section at the end of each book. You can also visit our website at <www.keswickministries.org/resources> to find the full range of books, study guides, CDs, DVDs and mp3s available. Why not order an audio recording of the Bible Reading series to accompany your daily devotional?

> *Let the word of Christ dwell in you richly.*
> (Colossians 3:16, ESV)

Introduction
Revelation

Does the church have a future?

Across the generations, troubled Christians have often asked this question.

Even as early as the end of the first century, the future of the church hung in the balance. False teaching, internal division and persecution were rife. Emperor Domitian had exiled the apostle John, probably in his nineties, on the island of Patmos. You can imagine John, Jesus' beloved disciple, pacing up and down the island at night, looking across the sea to the cities on the shore, wondering, 'Does the church have a future?'

Into this situation the Lord comes and makes these glorious revelations. He gives John this vision and tells him to write to the seven churches of Asia Minor, in the eastern part of the Roman Empire, in what is now Turkey. The first letter is to Ephesus, which was the first place the postman would come to when travelling from Patmos. Then the letters move round in a horseshoe, up from

Patmos to Smyrna, to Pergamum and through Thyatira, Sardis, Philadelphia and finally to Laodicea.

To each of these churches Jesus says, 'I know . . . I know your hopes and dreams, your faults and failings, your joys and sorrows, your temptations and frustrations.' Jesus knew each of these churches and so he could speak wisely and truthfully into each circumstance. He said some hard things to shake believers out of their apathy. He also spoke words of comfort: 'I am with you. I am going to bring a new world where there will be no pain or sorrow.' Every letter ends by pointing the believers to heaven, a reminder that despite their present struggles, ultimately, they are on the victory side.

Like those first-century believers, we have so many spiritual blessings in Christ, but at the same time we still struggle with sin, failure, doubt and bereavement. Theologians describe this tension as living between 'the already and the not yet'. But John's glorious vision reminds us that we are on the victory side. When we trusted in Christ, when we were placed in Christ, we were put in a position of ultimate strength.

Today the church still faces internal division. Opposition from media and government is increasing. In various parts of the world the persecution of Christians is rife. In such testing times it is understandable that some believers question, 'Does the church have a future?'

The answer is the same as it has always been.

Absolutely.

Day 1

Read Revelation 1:1–20
Key verses: Revelation 1:13–16

....

> ¹³*Among the lampstands was someone like a son of man, dressed in a robe reaching down to his feet and with a golden sash round his chest.* ¹⁴*The hair on his head was white like wool, as white as snow, and his eyes were like blazing fire.* ¹⁵*His feet were like bronze glowing in a furnace, and his voice was like the sound of rushing waters.* ¹⁶*In his right hand he held seven stars, and coming out of his mouth was a sharp, double-edged sword. His face was like the sun shining in all its brilliance.*

'When I get to heaven I'm going to ask Jesus about . . .' We often speculate about the questions to which we will finally receive answers when we meet Jesus.

However, the apostle John's experience suggests that talking will be the last thing on our minds.

Revelation begins with this vision of the awesome majesty of Christ. John can barely describe it and he uses the word 'like' or 'as' seven times. He says, 'When I saw him, I fell at his feet as though dead' (verse 17). Jesus is not now the babe of Bethlehem, the pale Galilean, or the man of Calvary bathed in blood. He is King of kings and Lord of lords, the strong Son of God. He is magnificent, glorious and majestic.

John was the beloved disciple, yet, as he looks at Jesus, he acknowledges there is an awesomeness about him, a terrifying otherness. When we look at Jesus, we also see a terrible beauty about him. He is our friend but he is not our mate. He is the Holy One of God.

We live in a culture that has lost the fear of God, because the church has lost the fear of God. We no longer think of God as awesome, glorious and majestic. The Hebrew word for 'glory' can be described as the 'heaviness' of God. God is substantial, significant. We need to regain that sense of the awesome glory of Jesus. If the church is to endure suffering, trials and difficulties, we need to recapture this vision of Christ: the magnificent warrior, who will conquer his enemies and come for his people, is reigning now.

When was the last time you felt the awesomeness of God, his terrifying otherness? So often we domesticate and tame God, reducing him to manageable proportions. In doing so, we strip away his glory, majesty and the 'blazing fire' of his holiness. Our over-familiarity gives us a god we can handle, predict and control – a powerless, pygmy god.

Today, come into God's presence with reverence. Meditate on John's vision. Whatever your day holds, this is the God who is with you and for you. He is no longer the helpless baby in the Christmas card manger scene or the tortured figure on a cross. He is the King of kings and Lord of lords, the mighty warrior who is reigning now and will one day bring in the new heavens and new earth where you will take your place. Amen!

Day 2

Read Revelation 1:1–20
Key verses: Revelation 1:17–18

....

¹⁷When I saw him, I fell at his feet as though dead. Then he placed his right hand on me and said: 'Do not be afraid. I am the First and the Last. ¹⁸I am the Living One; I was dead, and now look, I am alive for ever and ever! And I hold the keys of death and Hades.'

Imagine the book of Revelation as a film.

This scene would be the first of many dramatic cliffhangers. The tension would be palpable. The Lord of glory appears in all his majestic brilliance, and John falls down at his feet, lying face down in the dirt. What happens next? What does Jesus do?

He stoops down from his throne and he lifts up his servant. He is the glorious merciful Saviour who stoops from the glory of heaven to lift sinners out of the dirt and put their feet on a rock. In Psalm 3:3 David refers to God as 'my glory, and the lifter of my head' (ESV). It is a picture of the ancient court where someone who had offended the king would be thrown on his face. If the king decided there would be no mercy, he would click his fingers and the man was taken out for execution. If the king decided to have mercy, he might point to one of his officers who would come and lift up the man's head so that he could see the king. But if the king wanted to demonstrate his forgiveness to the one who had offended him, he would leave his throne and come to where the man was in the dirt and would lift up his head. The first face the man would see would be that of the king.

You can look into the face of your King.

Jesus left his throne and all the splendour of heaven to come to earth. Our glorious King died on a cross to pay the penalty for our sins (Philippians 2:6–8). His death brings forgiveness and a restored relationship with God. It guarantees that you are welcome in his presence. He wants to hear your prayers, praises, concerns and adoration. So don't be afraid to draw near – come and stand on holy ground; gaze into the face of your King: 'Let us then approach God's throne of grace with confidence, so that we may receive mercy and find grace to help us in our time of need' (Hebrews 4:16).

Live for him today in thankful adoration.

Look to the LORD and his strength;
    seek his face always.
(Psalm 105:4)

Day 3

Read Revelation 2:1–7
Key verses: Revelation 2:1, 7

....

> [1] *To the angel of the church in Ephesus write:*
>
> > *These are the words of him who holds the seven stars in his right hand and walks among the seven golden lampstands . . .* [7] *Whoever has ears, let them hear what the Spirit says to the churches.*

Christians are often called 'People of the Book'. An apt description for past generations, but is it still applicable today?

Notice that each of the letters starts in the same way: verse 1, 'To the angel of the church in . . . write: These are the *words* . . .' And every one of the seven letters ends on the same note: verse 7, 'Whoever has ears, let them *hear what the Spirit says* to the churches' (italics mine). These phrases frame each letter.

What are the marks of being godly? One of the marks, and one of the needs of our spiritual renewal, is to be people who love the Word of God. What we have in our hands is the most precious physical object in the universe. This is the Word of the living God. What the Scriptures say, God says. But the purpose of God in speaking to us is not simply to entertain, enthral or even inform us. The purpose of the Word of God is to transform us.

God the Father is the author of renewal. His plan and purpose for our lives is that we might be holy: 'He chose us in him before the creation of the world to be holy and blameless in his sight' (Ephesians 1:4). Jesus Christ is the model of renewal, to become like Jesus is the goal of our lives, and the Holy Spirit is the agent of renewal. As we go through these letters, every one of them speaks of the ministry of the Spirit: 'Hear what the Spirit says to the churches.' But the Word of God is the instrument of renewal. If we are to be renewed in the power of God to be the kind of people he wants us to be, then we have to listen to what God says to us through his Word.

Do you struggle to spend time in God's Word? When our to-do list is long, sometimes it feels self-indulgent to take time to read the Bible. We forget that this is not a luxury, but a fundamental necessity for our spiritual life and growth. Make every effort to drown out distracting voices and soak in God's Word – study it, memorize it, meditate on it and share it with others.

Let God's Word become your source of strength, joy, comfort and direction, as Psalm 119 describes:

How can a young person stay on the path of purity?
  By living according to your word.
(verse 9)

My soul is weary with sorrow;
  strengthen me according to your word.
(verse 28)

I run in the path of your commands,
  for you have broadened my understanding.
(verse 32)

Your word is a lamp for my feet,
  a light on my path.
(verse 105)

You are my refuge and my shield;
  I have put my hope in your word.
(verse 114)

Day 4

Read Revelation 2:1–7
Key verses: Revelation 2:2–3

••

²I know your deeds, your hard work and your perseverance. I know that you cannot tolerate wicked people, that you have tested those who claim to be apostles but are not, and have found them false. ³You have persevered and have endured hardships for my name, and have not grown weary.

It was nicknamed the Light of Asia.

The city of Ephesus was the most important of the seven cities, famous for its banks, boulevards and harbour. It was a melting pot of people from all over the Roman Empire. People came specifically to worship at the Temple of Artemis (or Diana), one of the wonders of the world (Acts 19).

In this demon-infested, immoral city, the church shone as a bright light. It had been founded by the apostle Paul in around AD 52 as part of his third missionary journey, and he spent two years there. Ten years later he wrote the letter to the Ephesians, the crown of his theology. Timothy pastored the Ephesian church, and Paul wrote 1 and 2 Timothy to him while he was there. According to tradition, John the apostle, who wrote Revelation, also pastored the church at Ephesus.

Perhaps, then, it is not surprising that Christ commends the church. It was –

• A busy church

Verse 2: 'I know your deeds, your hard work.' The Greek word conveys the idea of labouring to the point of exhaustion. It is good to be a busy church. If you are saved, you are set aside for service. Indeed, the role of the pastor/teacher is not just to do the ministry, but to prepare God's people for works of service (Ephesians 4:12). Every Christian has a gift that is given by Christ for the glory of God and for the building up of the church. Whoever you are, whatever gift you have, it is for the good of the church, and you are needed.

• A discerning church

They vehemently opposed false teachers (verse 2). In verse 6 the sentiment is even stronger: 'But you have this in your favour: you hate the practices of the Nicolaitans, which I also hate.' This church knew that truth was important.

• A steadfast church

The Christians had endured hardships and persecution (verse 3). They had seen their pastor, John, thrown into prison, but had not given up.

Are you busy in God's service? Church is not supposed to be like a football match where the majority of us sit in the stands cheering on the active few. God has placed you, with your particular gifts, in your local church (Romans 12:6–8; 1 Corinthians 12; 1 Peter 4:10–11). Of course, church isn't the only place where we serve God, but it is certainly a starting point. Will you find out how you can use your gift in the life of the church? If you are already serving, will you persevere? You may not be recognized or thanked by others, but the Lord knows all your work on his behalf. Determine to wait patiently for his reward (Matthew 16:27; 1 Corinthians 3:10–15).

Day 5

Read Revelation 2:1–7
Key verse: Revelation 2:4

. . . .

⁴Yet I hold this against you: you have forsaken the love you had at first.

It must be one of the most devastating statements in the whole of Scripture: 'You have left your first love' (NKJV).

One person translates it: 'You do not love me as much as you used to. You have given up loving me.' When the church was planted in AD 52, it had been on fire for God. When Paul wrote the letter to the Ephesians in AD 62, about thirty years before the book of Revelation was penned, it was a church that had a reputation for love (Ephesians 1:15; 6:24). But now that love has grown cold. You can imagine the Christians there saying, 'We are tired out. Have you seen all our church ministries? Haven't you seen our programme? We are fighting for truth. We have suffered for your name.' 'Yes,' says the Lord, 'but you do not love me like you used to. You can have all those things, but if your love has grown cold, then it is fatal.'

Sometimes we are so busy about the Lord's service that we do not have time for the Lord we serve. The issue is worship. Of course, worship is everything we do: it is 24/7, presenting our bodies as living sacrifices to God. We worship God in the office, in the factory, when we are looking after the kids, struggling with pain and dealing with elderly relatives. The New Testament talks about worship in this broad sense, but it also speaks about those moments we spend gazing on God. We are to come, as individuals or as the body of Christ, and spend time gazing on the beauty of the Lord, declaring his worth, delighting in his character, loving him, adoring him, praising his name, surrendering our will to him.

In verse 4 we are assuming that the love that is spoken of is a love for Christ, but it could equally be a love for God's people. When we fall out of love with the Lord, we find God's people very hard to love. The only thing that sustains a ministry of loving difficult people is the love of Christ. We cannot love the church unless we love Christ.

Are you bitter as you look around at those in the church who don't work as hard as you do? Do you find yourself criticizing others or feeling overprotective of your ministry? Do you feel exhausted and joyless in serving? Perhaps, like the Ephesians, you have become so busy in the Lord's service that you have forgotten the Lord you serve. God is jealous for your love. It doesn't matter how much you serve, how well you know your Bible, or how many spiritual victories you have experienced in the past, if you don't love the Lord wholeheartedly. Do you love God more now than you did six months, a year or even ten years ago? Are you grieving the Lord? If so, acknowledge his rebuke, repent and ask forgiveness:

Today, if you hear his voice,
do not harden your hearts.
(Hebrews 4:7)

Day 6

Read Revelation 2:1–7
Key verses: Revelation 2:5, 7

....

> [5]*Consider how far you have fallen! Repent and do the things you did at first. If you do not repent, I will come to you and remove your lampstand from its place . . .* [7]*Whoever has ears, let them hear what the Spirit says to the churches. To the one who is victorious, I will give the right to eat from the tree of life, which is in the paradise of God.*

Is it possible to recapture the passionate, zealous love for God you had when you were a new Christian?

Absolutely! The living Christ urges these Ephesian Christians, 'Consider how far you have fallen.' Bring it to mind and hold it there. Remember when you first became a Christian. Remember how you fell in love with Jesus. Remember it; keep dwelling on it. Then 'repent' – this is a sudden, urgent turning to Christ. And he says, 'Do the things you did at first.' In other words, go back to living as you did when you first became a Christian; go back to doing the same things. Can you remember when you first fell in love with Jesus, when you first went to the cross? Go back to that point – to the primitive, unsophisticated simplicity of that first love.

He gives them two encouragements to go back to that simplicity. One is negative, one positive. The negative one is in verse 5: if you do not do something about it, you will have no future. The positive one in verse 7 is a promise of paradise. The word 'paradise' appears three times in the New Testament. It is used when Jesus is speaking to the thief on the cross (Luke 23:43), and Paul uses it in 2 Corinthians 12. This Persian word refers to a garden of delight.

How do I get this first love back? You can't manufacture it; you can only look at his love for you. When was the last time you looked at that Calvary love and it broke your heart and showed you how much you love your Saviour?

Do you ever wonder how much God loves you? God the Father devised the plan of salvation whereby he sent his only Son to the cross for us. Surely we must agree with John: 'See what great love the Father has lavished on us' (1 John 3:1). And Christ willingly died on the cross to rescue us from our sin and adopt us as sons and daughters of God. Today, gaze on that breathtaking Calvary love.

Man of sorrows, what a name
for the Son of God, who came
ruined sinners to reclaim:
Hallelujah, what a Saviour!

Bearing shame and scoffing rude,
in my place condemned he stood,
sealed my pardon with his blood:
Hallelujah, what a Saviour!

Guilty, helpless, lost were we;
blameless Lamb of God was he,
sacrificed to set us free:
Hallelujah, what a Saviour!

He was lifted up to die;
'It is finished' was his cry;
now in heaven exalted high:
Hallelujah, what a Saviour!
(Philip P. Bliss, 1875)

Day 7

Read Revelation 2:8–11
Key verses: Revelation 2:9–10

....

> [9]*I know your afflictions and your poverty – yet you are rich! I know about the slander of those who say they are Jews and are not, but are a synagogue of Satan.* [10]*Do not be afraid of what you are about to suffer. I tell you, the devil will put some of you in prison to test you, and you will suffer persecution for ten days. Be faithful, even to the point of death, and I will give you life as your victor's crown.*

The devil hates you, your Christian faith, your marriage, your kids, your church, your pastor.

The believers in Smyrna knew they had to take the devil seriously. They lived in a beautiful city. It was, according to legend, founded by the Greeks and was the birthplace of Homer, the father of Western literature. It was wealthy due to an exclusive right to import myrrh – an anaesthetic in great demand in the ancient world. And it was nicknamed the resurrection city because twice in its history it had been destroyed and had, metaphorically, risen out of the ashes. Interestingly, when Jesus introduces himself to this city, he describes himself as the one who has risen from the dead.

But Smyrna was a dangerous city for Christians. The Roman Empire was huge and covered most of the known world. Loyalty was cultivated by emperor worship. At least once a year every Roman citizen had to go into the temple and burn incense, confessing that the emperor was Lord and God. But the Christians refused. Their backs were against the wall, and the people who were informing on them were from the synagogue. Jews were exempt from emperor worship, but they claimed that the Christians were an upstart sect and encouraged Emperor Domitian to take severe measures against them.

Christ tells these Christians in Smyrna that Satan is going to throw some of them into prison; they're going to be persecuted by the Roman Empire. But behind the Roman Empire is Satan. We often think that the devil is a tame little beast whom we can pat on the head. But he is highly intelligent, immensely powerful, remarkably persistent, fiendishly cunning, violently malicious and utterly un-scrupulous. He can attack your mind and body. He can bring persecution and false teaching. He will do everything he can to destroy your Christian faith.

Right now, the devil is prowling around you. He is looking for your weak spots, areas where you are prone to temptation, any way he can get a foothold on your life (Ephesians 4:27; 1 Peter 5:8). Stand firm and resist the devil's schemes by putting on each element of the armour of God (Ephesians 6:10–18). Most importantly, remember whom you belong to:

> I'm not afraid of the devil. The devil can handle me – he's got judo I never heard of. But he can't handle the One to whom I'm joined; he can't handle the One to whom I'm united; he can't handle the One whose nature dwells in my nature.
>
> (A. W. Tozer, *Gems from Tozer*, Moody Press, 1980)

Day 8

Read Revelation 2:8–11

Key verse: Revelation 2:9

....

⁹I know your afflictions and your poverty – yet you are rich! I know about the slander of those who say they are Jews and are not, but are a synagogue of Satan.

Does God want Christians to be happy, healthy and prosperous?

If he does, you might imagine you would have found them in the wealthy, influential city of Smyrna. But the church was a small, struggling, frail bunch of people. The Christians at Smyrna were insignificant, downtrodden, despised and threadbare.

Notice the words that Jesus uses to describe them in verse 9:

• Affliction

The Greek word *thlipsis* is used, frequently translated as 'persecution' or 'torture'. These believers in Smyrna were facing the weight, the relentless pressure, of persecution.

• Poverty

There are different Greek words to describe poverty. The one used here conveys the sense of having nothing at all. This was a destitute church in an affluent community. Probably many of them were slaves or had been ostracized for their faith. There are those who say that if you're a Christian, you should never be sick or have any problems. You should be wealthy and prosperous. But sometimes, in the mystery of God's providence, the choicest Christians go through affliction and suffering.

• Slander

Slander comes from those who are the 'synagogue of Satan'. Much of the persecution, certainly in the Acts of the Apostles, came from the Jewish direction. Not all those who are Israel are real Israel. True Jews are not those descended from Abraham, but those who have faith in Christ.

Given the church's circumstances, you might think these Christians were being punished for some grievous sin. But this is the shortest and warmest of all the letters. No faults or criticisms are mentioned. I'm sure Smyrna wasn't a perfect church, and yet this was a letter of unconditional commendation. Christ's message to these struggling believers was that he knew and loved them.

Don't let difficult circumstances cause you to doubt God's love. You are infinitely precious to him. He delights in you. Seek his purpose and plans even in dark days (Ephesians 3:14–19).

Do you think anyone is going to be able to drive a wedge between us and Christ's love for us? There is no way! Not trouble, not hard times, not hatred, not hunger, not homelessness, not bullying threats, not back-stabbing, not even the worst sins listed in Scripture . . . None of this fazes us because Jesus loves us. I'm absolutely convinced that nothing – nothing living or dead, angelic or demonic, today or tomorrow, high or low, thinkable or unthinkable – absolutely *nothing* can get between us and God's love because of the way that Jesus our Master has embraced us.

(Romans 8:35–39, MSG)

Day 9

Read Revelation 2:8–11
Key verse: Revelation 2:9

....

⁹I know your afflictions and your poverty – yet you are rich! I know about the slander of those who say they are Jews and are not, but are a synagogue of Satan.

What makes a person rich?

Surprisingly, Christ says that the church in Smyrna was rich. They were being persecuted, but, in God's eyes, these poor, pitiful Christians were rich.

Can I remind you of the spiritual riches you have in Christ? You have been justified. God has declared you righteous in his sight. You are as righteous as a redeemed sinner ever can be. You will always be righteous and justified in his sight. You are being sanctified – no matter how stubborn you are, the Holy Spirit won't give up on you. He is sanctifying you, and you will be glorified. God, the

Creator and Sustainer of the universe, is your Father, King, Master, shield and hiding place. He provides, guides and protects you.

Jesus, the Son of God, lives in you, loves you and prays for you. He is your Brother, Saviour, Lord and Friend. He will never let you go. The Holy Spirit seals you: he is the life of God in the soul of man. He gives assurance, comfort, encouragement and joy. You have an inheritance that will never perish, fade or disappoint, and it's reserved in heaven for you. You are the child of a king, a soldier in his army, a stone in his temple and a sheep in his flock. You have brothers and sisters who love, encourage, support and pray for you. You have the Word of God in your hand and in your heart. It feeds, guides and brings you light in the darkness. It gives you purpose, direction and a goal for your life.

You look up and there's no judgment. You look down and there's no hell. You look in and the peace of God that passes all understanding guards your heart and mind. You look back and your sins are covered. You look forward and the glory dawns in the future because Jesus is coming back for you. You are saved, sealed, satisfied, secured and destined for glory!

You might not have a big bank balance or great career prospects, but you are rich. God has blessed you with every spiritual blessing in Christ (Ephesians 1:3). He has lavished his love upon you, given you a peace that cannot be bought, joy that does not depend on mood or circumstance, and an inheritance that can never run out. The riches you have are unsurpassable, incomparable and inexhaustible. Are you living like a person who is rich in Christ?

Today, be generous with your time and finances, find your confidence and security in Christ, don't fear for the future, trust God for your needs, share the good news of the gospel with someone and be thankful: 'My God will meet all your needs according to the riches of his glory in Christ Jesus' (Philippians 4:19).

Day 10

Read Revelation 2:8–11
Key verse: Revelation 2:8

....

8 *To the angel of the church in Smyrna write:*

These are the words of him who is the First and the Last, who died and came to life again.

When you are suffering, what do you need to know? What truths, what hope do you need to cling to?

The first thing Christ says to the church in Smyrna facing persecution is: 'I am alive.'

Here are the two great facts of Christian history: Christ died once and for all on the cross, and he rose again from the dead. The resurrection is an indisputable historical fact. It is not a symbol, myth or parable; it is a physical, literal and datable event. Of course, it's interesting that John, who wrote this book, was one of the very first to believe the resurrection. In John's account, in chapter 20 of his Gospel, the disciples hear the news from Mary, and John and Peter run to the tomb. John gets there first. That simple fact authenticates the historical relevance and reliability of the story. He arrived at the empty tomb first because he was there on the spot. He didn't even see the risen Christ. He saw the folded grave clothes and was utterly convinced of the resurrection.

The resurrection is not only an indisputable fact of history, but also has massive significance for our lives. Just look back at Revelation 1:17:

> When I saw him, I fell at his feet as though dead. Then he placed his right hand on me and said: 'Do not be afraid. I am the First and the Last. I am the Living One; I was dead, and now look, I am alive for ever and ever! And I hold the keys of death and Hades.'

What a comfort to know that death is not the end. If you have to go through the veil of death, Jesus is on the other side. Jesus, the Lord of glory, has conquered death and has risen. He now holds the keys of the grave and can unlock it for all his people. When we have to face death, and even when we have to face death for the sake of the gospel, it's wonderful to proclaim that Jesus is alive.

Why are we so afraid when we think about death? . . . Death is only dreadful for those who live in dread and fear of it. Death is not wild and terrible, if only we can be still and hold fast to God's Word. Death is not bitter, if we have not become bitter ourselves.

Death is grace, the greatest gift of grace that God gives to people who believe in him. Death is mild, death is sweet and gentle; it beckons to us with heavenly power, if only we realize that it is the gateway to our homeland, the tabernacle of joy, the everlasting kingdom of peace.

How do we know that dying is so dreadful? Who knows whether in our human fear and anguish we are only shivering and shuddering at the most glorious, heavenly, blessed event in the world?

Death is hell and night and cold, if it is not transformed by our faith. But that is just what is so marvellous, that we can transform death.

(Eric Metaxas, *Bonhoeffer: Pastor, Martyr, Prophet, Spy*, Thomas Nelson, 2010, p. 531)

Day 11

Read Revelation 2:8–11
Key verses: Revelation 2:9–10

....

> [9]*I know your afflictions and your poverty – yet you are rich! I know about the slander of those who say they are Jews and are not, but are a synagogue of Satan.* [10]*Do not be afraid of what you are about to suffer. I tell you, the devil will put some of you in prison to test you, and you will suffer persecution for ten days. Be faithful, even to the point of death, and I will give you life as your victor's crown.*

When we look at our world, and even at our own lives, we may wonder who is in control.

Jesus wanted the church in Smyrna to know that, although the devil was going to put some believers in prison, God was the one calling the shots. Their imprisonment is not an accident. God is not on the sidelines, ringing his hands, saying, 'I'd love to help you but I can't.' No, he is saying, 'I'm in control. The devil will attack you, but it's only part of my purpose and plan.'

The doctrine of the sovereignty of a loving God is the single most comforting doctrine we can possibly have as Christians. We may think of it as a harsh and difficult doctrine, but that is not the case at all. Christ reigns, and I'm in his hands. Whatever I have to go through – even if I suffer death, even if I am persecuted – I'm not in the hands of human beings; I'm in the hands of Jesus. My suffering may be for ten days, which is a limited period, but he will call the shots. He'll start it and he'll finish it.

Whatever you are going through today, God has a purpose in it. The devil might be testing you to destroy you. But God tests you in order to make you strong. Imagine I'm walking along the road and I pick up a lump of rock. There is a seam in it that appears to be gold. What do I do? I crush it and put it in the furnace to extract the pure gold. Why? Not because it's worthless, but because it has value. God looks at our lives and sees the gold of holiness. He crushes us and puts us in the furnace. He produces something that lasts. Whatever trials you are going through today, remember that God is in control and he knows what he's doing.

There is nothing – no circumstance, no trouble, no testing – that can ever touch me until, first of all, it has gone past God and past Christ right through to me. If it has come that far, it has come with a great purpose, which I may not understand at the moment. But as I refuse to become panicky, as I lift up my eyes to Him and accept it as coming from the throne of God for some great purpose of blessing to my own heart, no sorrow will ever disturb me, no trial will ever disarm me, no circumstance will cause me to fret – for I shall rest in the joy of what my Lord is! That is the rest of victory!
(Alan Redpath, quoted in Elizabeth George, *Loving God with All Your Mind*, Harvest House Publishers, 2005, p. 204)

Day 12

Read Revelation 2:8–11
Key verse: Revelation 2:11

....

[11]Whoever has ears, let them hear what the Spirit says to the churches. The one who is victorious will not be hurt at all by the second death.

If we send a text or an email to someone who is dealing with a difficult situation, we usually try to end on a positive, hopeful note.

Strangely, perhaps, Jesus did not end his letter to the church in Smyrna with warm words of blessing. Instead, his parting comment to the believers was a reminder that they were not going to hell. They would not be hurt by the second death, the death after death. We struggle with this doctrine of eternal, conscious separation from God. It's intellectually demanding, emotionally draining and morally disturbing. We say, 'Well, that's the God of the Old Testament, the God of wrath, not the God of the New Testament.' But Jesus talked more about hell than anyone else. He spoke about darkness, weeping and gnashing of teeth. He spoke about the two gates, two roads, two crowds and two destinies. It was Jesus who said it was better to pluck out your eye or cut off your hand than fall into hell.

The truth here is a simple reminder of the awesome seriousness of sin. The gravity of sin is seen most clearly and demonstrated most vividly when Christ, the holy Son of God, received the just punishment for our sins at Calvary. If you have any doubts about hell, look at the cross. Jesus says to these believers facing persecution – and it's a strange thing to say – in the end, just rejoice in the fact that you are saved from hell, at measureless cost.

Every single person you meet today is going to live for ever. Every single face you look into today will live for ever, either in heaven or in hell. What makes the difference? The gospel. Whatever we go through in this world, if we're Christians, we're going to glory – and that's wonderful.

At first it seems strange that Jesus would encourage persecuted believers by saying they would be spared hell. But, on reflection, how wise of Jesus to place their suffering in the context of eternity. How kind of him to remind them that, in the end, the only thing that mattered was that their eternal destiny was secure.

> Therefore we do not lose heart. Though outwardly we are wasting away, yet inwardly we are being renewed day by day. For our light and momentary troubles are achieving for us an eternal glory that far outweighs them all. So we fix our eyes not on what is seen, but on what is unseen, since what is seen is temporary, but what is unseen is eternal.
>
> (2 Corinthians 4:16–18)

Today, give thanks to God that, because of Jesus' sacrifice, you are headed for glory. Pray that God would use your life, witness and words to help point others heavenward. Look for an opportunity to share the gospel with someone you meet today.

Day 13

Read Revelation 2:12–17
Key verses: Revelation 2:12–13

....

¹² *To the angel of the church in Pergamum write:*

> *These are the words of him who has the sharp, double-edged sword. ¹³I know where you live – where Satan has his throne. Yet you remain true to my name. You did not renounce your faith in me, not even in the days of Antipas, my faithful witness, who was put to death in your city – where Satan lives.*

Would you die for your faith? That's the question facing the believers in Pergamum.

Historically, Pergamum was the capital city. The proconsul, or governor of the Roman province, lived there. When he went down the street, a man would walk in front of him carrying a sword as a symbol of his authority. Interestingly, when Jesus writes to this church, he reminds them that he holds the double-edged sword. He is the one with ultimate authority.

Paganism was thriving in Pergamum. On the hillside, overshadowing the whole city, was a massive altar to the Greek god Zeus. The patron god of the city was Asclepius, the god of healing. The symbol of Asclepius was a snake on a stick. Wherever you went in the city, there were images of serpents, and emperor worship was ubiquitous. The devil seemed to be rampant in this city, and the forces of evil overwhelming.

Paganism and persecution were a stage further on compared to what was happening in Smyrna. Believers weren't just being thrown into prison; Antipas, who was probably the pastor of the church, had been killed (verse 13). According to the church historian Eusebius, he was arrested for his faith, put inside a bronze bull and roasted alive.

What is the reason for this persecution? Verse 13 says, 'You remain true to my name.' But why are we hated as Christians? Not because we are religious in a general sense – the world can put up with that. It's because we believe that Jesus Christ is the only way to God; the only name under heaven by which we can be saved; the one revelation of God that is full, final and climactic. We are faithful to his name.

To the world this is scandalous. And if, like the Christians in Pergamum, you stand up for this truth and are faithful to God's name, you'll face opposition too.

We shouldn't be surprised if we suffer for being a Christian – missing out on a promotion, being ostracized by family or mocked by the media (John 15:18–25). The signs indicate that in our generation persecution will become increasingly overt in the West. We may not have to die for our faith, but we will experience the cost of discipleship. Today, pray for wisdom to represent Christ well and be faithful to his name in your particular circumstances.

Pray too for believers around the world who are suffering, one of whom, a Middle Eastern Christian woman, urged,

Don't pray for the persecution to be stopped . . . But pray for the Christians, for their boldness, their encouragement, for their faith and that they can all be witnesses for God's work and for God.

(*Christian Times*, 11 August 2016, <www.christiantimes. com/article/dont-pray-for-the-persecution-to-be-stopped>)

Day 14

Read Revelation 2:12–17
Key verse: Revelation 2:14

....

14 Nevertheless, I have a few things against you: there are some among you who hold to the teaching of Balaam, who taught Balak to entice the Israelites to sin so that they ate food sacrificed to idols and committed sexual immorality.

'The long, dull, monotonous years of middle-aged prosperity or middle-aged adversity are excellent campaigning weather for the devil' (C. S. Lewis, *The Screwtape Letters*, William Collins, 2016, p. 155).

The devil doesn't always attack us with persecution. In fact, a more subtle method of seduction is usually more effective, whatever age we are!

It certainly worked in the church at Pergamum. 'Balaam' is a code word that takes us back to Numbers 22 – 25. The Israelites had come out of the Promised Land and had conquered all their enemies. They come to the plains of Moab, and the king, Balak, realizes that his time is up. So he sends for the prophet Balaam to curse the Israelites so that he could defeat them in battle.

The plan backfires and, instead of cursing Israel, he blesses them. Balaam explains to the king that attacking the Israelites won't work; he needs another plan. So, when the Israelites come to a place called Baal Peor, the beautiful women of Moab seduce them. They begin to worship idols and commit fornication, and God's wrath falls upon them.

Do you see, seduction is far more dangerous to the church than persecution? When the church is persecuted, very often it grows and flourishes. The second-century Church Father Tertullian said, 'The blood of the martyrs is the seed of the church.' But when the devil joins the church and seduces it with false teaching, it is in real danger.

Remember King David? When the devil attacked him, he just grew stronger and wrote some wonderful psalms. It is in middle age, when he is relaxing at home instead of going to war, that the devil is able to seduce him with the beautiful Bathsheba. He takes her, and his reign is ruined. God forgives him, but the implications go on and on.

The Lord says to this church, 'If you don't stand against this seduction and deal with false teaching and immorality, I'm going to come against you with the sword of my mouth.' Jesus, the divine Warrior, will fight for the purity of his church.

> We are too apt to forget that temptation to sin will rarely present itself to us in its true colours saying, 'I am your deadly enemy, and I want to ruin you forever in hell.' Oh no! Sin comes to us like Judas, with a kiss; like Joab, with an outstretched hand and flattering words. The forbidden fruit seemed good and desirable to Eve; yet it cast her out of Eden. Walking idly on his palace roof seemed harmless enough to David; yet it ended in adultery and murder. Sin rarely seems [like] sin at first beginnings. Let us watch and pray, lest we fall into temptation.
>
> (J. C. Ryle, *Holiness*, 1877, Ichthus Publications, 2017, p. 7)

Where are your weak points, those areas where you're particularly susceptible to the devil's schemes? Will you pray for strength to resist and actively root out sin?

Day 15

Read Revelation 2:12–17
Key verse: Revelation 2:13

. . . .

13 I know where you live – where Satan has his throne. Yet you remain true to my name. You did not renounce your faith in me, not even in the days of Antipas, my faithful witness, who was put to death in your city – where Satan lives.

Do you know that Christians sometimes lie?

They tell more lies on a Sunday morning at the end of a service than at any other time. The pastor shakes your hand and asks, 'How are you doing?' And you say, 'Fine.' Your life is falling apart. Nobody knows the problems you are having at work. Nobody knows that although you have been widowed many years, you still miss your husband every day. Nobody knows the problems in your marriage, yet no other Christian couples seem to be struggling. Nobody knows about the problems you are having with your children. Everybody else's kids seem to be perfect Christians.

But Jesus knows.

In verse 13 he says to the church, 'I *know* where you live.' Back in verse 9 he said, 'I *know* your afflictions and your poverty . . . I *know* about the slander' (italics mine). This isn't the knowledge of observation; it is the knowledge of experience. To put it in a simple way, when we look at those words in verse 9 – affliction, poverty, slander – we could be talking about the earthly ministry of Jesus. He was afflicted on the cross more than any other person. He knew poverty: 'Foxes have dens . . . but the Son of Man has nowhere to lay his head' (Matthew 8:20). He was slandered. People said he was mad and demon-possessed. When Jesus says, 'I *know*', this isn't the knowledge of a distant, removed God. This is the knowledge of a high priest who's been where you are, who looks and sees and knows your sorrows, who is tenderly moved by the concerns and sufferings of his people.

Perhaps nobody else knows your pain. What a comfort that Jesus knows. He's been bruised and broken. He is the man of sorrows, acquainted with grief (Isaiah 53:3).

Whatever your heartache . . . Jesus knows.

I could never believe in God, if it were not for the cross . . . that lonely, twisted, tortured figure on the cross, nails through hands and feet, back lacerated, limbs wrenched, brow bleeding from thorn pricks, mouth dry and intolerably thirsty, plunged into God-forsaken darkness. That is the God for me! He laid aside his immunity to pain. He entered our world of flesh and blood, tears and death. He suffered for us. Our sufferings become more manageable in the light of his. There is still a question mark against human suffering, but over it we boldly stamp another mark, the cross which symbolizes divine suffering.

(John Stott, *The Cross of Christ*, IVP, 1986, pp. 335–336)

Day 16

Read Revelation 2:18–29
Key verse: Revelation 2:18

....

¹⁸ *To the angel of the church in Thyatira write:*

These are the words of the Son of God, whose eyes are like blazing fire and whose feet are like burnished bronze.

What happens when our Christian principles clash with society's expectations?

For the believers in Thyatira this was a daily struggle.

The city was a military colony founded by Alexander the Great. The soldiers worshipped the Greek god Apollo, who had been given the title, 'The son of god'. It was also a commercial centre. In Acts 16 Paul speaks about Lydia, the first European convert, a dealer in purple, who came from Thyatira. The city was famous for its trade guilds, and the only way you could get a job was by joining a guild. Each trade guild dedicated a banquet once a month to their patron god. The health of the god was toasted, and burnt offerings were dedicated to the image of the god. Usually these sessions would end with an orgy. Of course, Christians were forbidden from eating food offered to idols, or indulging in immorality or fornication, so how could they live and work in a city where they were constantly being asked to go against their moral scruples?

Christ's response is to give these distraught believers a magnificent insight into who he is (verse 18). Apollo, the son of Zeus, is not the son of god; he's just a passing image. Jesus is Lord and King. Truly, he is the Son of God, glorious in majesty.

His eyes are like blazing fire, signifying his absolute justice, inflexible integrity and supernatural knowledge. When you look into the face of Jesus, you lay yourself bare before him. His eyes see everything in your soul. We can't hide anything from him.

His feet are like burnished bronze. That's a picture of his strength, power and majesty. It is echoed in Ezekiel's vision of the glory of God. When he stands firm, nothing is going to move him. From head to toe, he is the glorious Son of God.

When you read all the books John wrote – his Gospel, the book of Revelation and his three letters – the theme of the absolute deity of Jesus is underlined again and again. Christ's message to these first believers, and to us, is that he is the co-equal, co-eternal Son of God. He is fully divine.

Today, as you face temptations to compromise your faith and opportunities to stand up for your beliefs, reflect on John's vision of Christ. His searching eyes are the only ones you should fear. His assessment of you is the only one that really counts. As you stand firm, remember you are resting your whole weight on the Son of God. The one with burnished bronze feet is strong enough to carry you, and stable enough to hold you fast:

Listen to me . . .
you whom I have upheld since your birth,
    and have carried since you were born.
Even to your old age and grey hairs
    I am he, I am he who will sustain you.
I have made you and I will carry you;
    I will sustain you and I will rescue you.
(Isaiah 46:3–4)

Day 17

Read Revelation 2:18–29
Key verse: Revelation 2:19

. . . .

19 I know your deeds, your love and faith, your service and perseverance, and that you are now doing more than you did at first.

How would people describe your church? What are the standout characteristics?

If you went to the church at Thyatira, the first thing you would notice was that it was a wonderfully loving church. The Christians loved one another and they loved to talk about the Lord.

The foundations of this church were love and faith, which resulted in service and perseverance (verse 19). In other words, the believers had a love that led to service, and a faith that led to perseverance.

Love is crucial in a church. There is not one of the twenty-one letters or epistles of the New Testament written to the early church that doesn't speak about relationships between Christians. The sublime book of Romans deals with relationships between Christians of strong and weak faith. The book of Philemon is written to a slave owner, reminding him that Christianity affects his relationship with his slave now. Whichever book it is, each one speaks about relationships, because the biggest destructive force in churches is disunity amongst brothers and sisters.

Jesus commends this church because they have a wonderful love which leads to wonderful service. The word for 'service' is *diakonia*, conveying the idea of humble service – washing one another's feet or cleaning tables. Real love means getting your hands dirty.

Christ also commends this church for their faith. Saving faith is passive. We receive salvation as a free gift of grace from God. As the hymn writer says, 'Nothing in my hand I bring; simply to thy cross I cling' (Augustus Toplady, 'Rock of Ages', 1885). But living faith is always seen. In Hebrews 12 the proof or evidence that these great men had faith was seen by what they did. Faith works. Vision leads to venture. In Thyatira faith leads to wonderful perseverance. The believers don't give up.

What a commendation!

What is your church known for? Is it like Thyatira, known for love and active faith? Or is it like Ephesus, strict on doctrine but lacking in love? The right theology is important, but it is worth little if not accompanied by love. The New Testament is full of reminders about how we should treat one another – bear with one another, forgive one another, be patient and gentle . . . 'And over all these virtues put on love, which binds them all together in perfect unity' (Colossians 3:12–14).

Love is our hallmark: 'A new command I give you: love one another. As I have loved you, so you must love one another. By this everyone will know that you are my disciples, if you love one another' (John 13:34–35).

How will you show love to another Christian today?

Day 18

Read Revelation 2:18–29
Key verses: Revelation 2:20–23

....

> [20]*Nevertheless, I have this against you: you tolerate that woman Jezebel, who calls herself a prophet. By her teaching she misleads my servants into sexual immorality and the eating of food sacrificed to idols. [21]I have given her time to repent of her immorality, but she is unwilling. [22]So I will cast her on a bed of suffering, and I will make those who commit adultery with her suffer intensely, unless they repent of her ways. [23]I will strike her children dead. Then all the churches will know that I am he who searches hearts and minds, and I will repay each of you according to your deeds.*

In my years of ministry, I have learned that almost anyone is capable of almost anything, especially in relation to sin. And sin was rampant in the church at Thyatira.

Jezebel is another code word taking us back to 1 Kings 16. She was the wife of the wicked King Ahab and encouraged his idolatry. They set up an altar to Baal in the city of Samaria and sacrificed their children on it. They promoted immorality and cultic prostitution. Christ's point in referencing Jezebel is twofold:

• Truth is important.

As Christians, there can never be spiritual renewal in our lives, and in the church of Jesus, unless we are convicted and convinced about the truth of the great doctrines of the Christian faith. I don't mean that we become pernickety about secondary issues. But there are some things that are non-negotiable: the doctrine of the Trinity, the Incarnation, penal substitutionary atonement, the resurrection and the return of Christ. Indeed, the fundamental truth – the material principle of the Reformation – is *Sola Scriptura*, the authority of the Word of God. These believers were in trouble because they didn't confront false teaching. A mark of a church's truth and discipline is how it deals with falsehood.

• Lax teaching leads to lax living.

Jezebel was teaching that sin wasn't serious. This thinking affected the believers and led to immorality and idolatry.

We need to be clear in our thinking and recognize that all sin is vile. Lying is vile. Being unkind to your wife is vile. Internet pornography is vile. But God can forgive the vilest sin. The blood of Jesus is sufficient to cover your worst sin. Failure is not final. God can pour his grace into your life and give you deliverance.

John Bunyan described sin as taking your fist and smashing it into the face of Christ. When Jesus was arrested, the soldiers took him and put a blindfold over his eyes. Then, one after another, they came and smashed him in the face. When we sin, even as Christians, it's like that fist in the face of Jesus Christ.

Today, will you put a marker in the sand and deal with a particular sin you have been indulging in? Repent. Draw on God's strength to resist temptation. If it is helpful, pray specifically with a more mature Christian about this issue.

Day 19

Read Revelation 2:18–29
Key verses: Revelation 2:24–25

· ·

> [24] *Now I say to the rest of you in Thyatira, to you who do not hold to her teaching and have not learned Satan's so-called deep secrets, 'I will not impose any other burden on you,* [25] *except to hold on to what you have until I come.'*

Just keep on doing what you're doing. That was the message to the faithful believers in Thyatira.

In essence, what Christ is saying in verses 24–25 is this: 'I'm not going to give you any manmade rules or regulations. Just stick to the apostolic declaration. No immorality, no food offered to idols – just continue to strive to be holy.' Holiness is something we can never hope to achieve in our own strength. It is a work of God. It is also 100% our work. It isn't one or the other, but both at the same time. As Paul explains, 'Therefore, my dear friends . . . continue to work out your salvation with fear and trembling, for it is God who works in you to will and to act in order to fulfil his good purpose' (Philippians 2:12–13).

As the believers stay faithful and press on towards holiness, Christ holds out this great hope for the future: he's going to return (verse 25). He's going to rule 'with an iron sceptre' (verse 27), and 'I will also give that one the morning star' (verse 28). The morning star comes at the end of a dark night. If you are tossing and turning and can't sleep, when the star comes up you know that the morning is near. Christ reminds these struggling believers that the morning is near, and one of the great joys of heaven will be utter deliverance from sin.

Do you know why I'm looking forward to heaven? I will never ever sin again. Isn't that wonderful? Not only will I never sin again; I will never be able to sin again and I won't want to sin. I will be like Christ in all his holiness. As I struggle with sin every day, I look to Jesus, and I'm looking forward to that great day when the morning star rises, when I am with Christ and everything is well.

Don't be disheartened – the finishing line is in sight, the morning star is about to rise and your struggle with sin is almost over. In the short time remaining, pursue holiness as your primary ambition:

You need to persevere so that when you have done the will of God, you will receive what he has promised. For,

'In just a little while,
   he who is coming will come
   and will not delay.'
(Hebrews 10:36–37)

Therefore we do not lose heart. Though outwardly we are wasting away, yet inwardly we are being renewed day by day. For our light and momentary troubles are achieving for us an eternal glory that far outweighs them all. So we fix our eyes not on what is seen, but on what is unseen, since what is seen is temporary, but what is unseen is eternal.
(2 Corinthians 4:16–18)

Day 20

Read Revelation 3:1–6
Key verse: Revelation 3:1

• •

¹ *To the angel of the church in Sardis write:*

These are the words of him who holds the seven spirits of God and the seven stars. I know your deeds; you have a reputation of being alive, but you are dead.

Most of us would have liked to be a member of the church at Sardis. It was large, had a tremendous reputation, and everyone flocked to it: it was *the* place to be.

But despite this glorious history, the future was doubtful. The believers had a form of godliness but no power: they were dead. Similarly, the city's glory had faded. The old days of Sardis being a rich commercial centre were long gone. It had been conquered by enemies, had suffered an earthquake in AD 17, and now many of the buildings had crumbled and the shops were boarded up. There had been an attempt to build a temple to Diana to rival the one in Ephesus, but it had never been completed. The city, like the church, had a great beginning, but was not finishing well.

How does that happen? Why do churches with such great histories die? The introduction to the church in verse 1 helps to explain. It talks about the 'seven spirits'. Just as physical death is when the spirit leaves the body, so death in a church is the absence of the Holy Spirit.

Incidentally, 'seven spirits' does not mean that there are seven Holy Spirits. Revelation is a book of symbols, and seven is a symbol of perfection. The perfection of the living Spirit of God is in the hand of Jesus. Jesus, in his ascension, pours the Spirit upon the church, and so the church has been consumed and changed by the fire of God.

The problem at Sardis was that they had forgotten that we can do nothing without the power of the Holy Spirit.

Remember how God gave the Israelites manna in the desert? Apart from on the Sabbath, they were instructed to gather enough for each day (Exodus 16). Yesterday's manna rotted, so they had to trust God for a fresh supply each day. Just like the manna, there is a fresh supply of

God's grace, mercy and love each day. Don't rely on past experiences of the Holy Spirit, past answers to prayer, past study of God's Word to fuel your relationship with God. Don't be fooled that your family's history in the church or your reputation are any substitute for genuine discipleship. Today, come to God with a fresh hunger to hear his Word, a new passion to seek his face in prayer, and a renewed desire for his Spirit to reign in every area of your life.

> I am the vine; you are the branches. If you remain in me and I in you, you will bear much fruit; apart from me you can do nothing. If you do not remain in me, you are like a branch that is thrown away and withers; such branches are picked up, thrown into the fire and burned . . . This is to my Father's glory, that you bear much fruit, showing yourselves to be my disciples.
>
> (John 15:5–6, 8)

Day 21

Read Revelation 3:1–6
Key verses: Revelation 3:2–3

....

2Wake up! Strengthen what remains and is about to die, for I have found your deeds unfinished in the sight of my God. 3Remember, therefore, what you have received and heard; hold it fast, and repent. But if you do not wake up, I will come like a thief, and you will not know at what time I will come to you.

Do you sleepwalk?

Perhaps you did as a child. Today, many more of us sleepwalk our way through life, unconscious of all that is going on around us, giving little thought to our purpose or where we are heading.

The church at Sardis was sleepwalking. It was wedded to its tradition and nostalgia, and had no vision for the future. It is great to learn from the past, but we cannot dwell on it. The past is supposed to inspire us, not paralyse us, and if we do not change, we will die. Change is tough in church life. Of course, we never change the gospel. We cannot change it; it is not ours to change. But a lot of other things have to change.

Jesus says to the church in Sardis, 'You are sleepwalking into death! If you don't wake up and shape up, if you don't repent and deal with the issues in the church, if you don't strengthen the good things that remain, I will come like a thief and take the Holy Spirit from you. Then you will have no future at all.'

As the church of Jesus Christ, and as individual Christians, we need regularly to be filled with the Holy Spirit every day. The filling of the Spirit is an ongoing daily thing. 'Keep being filled,' says the apostle Paul (Ephesians 5:18). It is not as if we come to this little fountain with the cup of our life and we fill this little cup. Rather, we come with the cup of our life to a thousand Niagara Falls. We say, 'Lord, fill me today, because I need you. My work is difficult, my marriage is struggling, I don't know how to witness and I don't know how to cope – fill me.' And guess what happens? The great ocean of the fullness of the Spirit comes into our lives and overflows. Every moment of every day we need to be crying, 'Oh God, send your Spirit.'

Bring the cup of your life to God – your work, health, marriage, family, ministry, church – and pray that you would live in the power of the Holy Spirit today.

If you then, though you are evil, know how to give good gifts to your children, how much more will your Father in heaven give the Holy Spirit to those who ask him!
(Luke 11:13)

We continually ask God to fill you with the knowledge of his will through all the wisdom and understanding that the Spirit gives, so that you may live a life worthy of the Lord and please him in every way.
(Colossians 1:9–10)

The Spirit God gave us does not make us timid, but gives us power, love and self-discipline.
(2 Timothy 1:7)

Day 22

Read Revelation 3:1–6
Key verses: Revelation 3:4–5

. . . .

> [4] *Yet you have a few people in Sardis who have not soiled their clothes. They will walk with me, dressed in white, for they are worthy.* [5] *The one who is victorious will, like them, be dressed in white. I will never blot out the name of that person from the book of life, but will acknowledge that name before my Father and his angels.*

It is not easy staying faithful to God when those around you, especially those in the church, are compromising.

But be encouraged. God knows about you, just as he knew about the faithful few in Sardis. Notice that these people are dressed in white robes. In those days white robes were a symbol of festivity: when you were going to a celebration, you would put on white robes. They were robes of victory and purity, and most of all they were robes you wore to a wedding. When a Roman attended a wedding, he would dress in a white toga, just as today a bride puts on a white dress. But it is more than that.

White robes are a symbol, in John's thinking, of the righteousness of Christ. He is talking about the glorious doctrine of justification by faith. Justification is the work of God for us; it is a declaration that God sees us righteous in his sight because we are clothed in the pure and perfect righteousness of Christ. God justifies the ungodly. He blots out sin, and does not want you to remember what he has chosen to forget.

But that description of justification does not go far enough. Justification is a positive thing. God takes the righteousness of Christ and covers us with it. Remember when Jesus came out of the waters of baptism? His Father looked at him and said, 'This is my beloved Son, with whom I am well pleased' (Matthew 3:17, ESV). God was pleased with his perfect righteousness and utter obedience. Those robes of righteousness are laid on your shoulders today, and when God looks at you, he sees the glorious righteousness of Jesus. You are as right with God as you ever can be. It is instantaneous, it is legal, it is declarative and it is glorious. It is the gospel.

You are justified. How does, and should, this truth impact on your thought patterns and behaviour? This is John Bunyan's experience:

> But one day, as I was passing into a field . . . suddenly this sentence fell upon my soul, 'Thy righteousness is in heaven' . . . I saw with the eyes of my soul, Jesus Christ, at God's right hand; there, I say, is my righteousness; so that wherever I was, or whatever I was doing, God could not say 'He wants my righteousness,' for that was just before him. I also saw that it was not my good frame of heart that made my righteousness better; or my bad frame of heart that made it worse; for my righteousness was Jesus Christ himself, 'the same yesterday, and today, and forever'.
> (Hugh T. Kerr and John M. Mulder, *Famous Conversions*, Eerdmans, 1994, p. 79)

Give thanks for this glorious gospel of grace.

Day 23

Read Revelation 3:7–13
Key verses: Revelation 3:8, 11

....

8I know your deeds. See, I have placed before you an open door that no one can shut. I know that you have little strength, yet you have kept my word and have not denied my name . . . 11I am coming soon. Hold on to what you have, so that no one will take your crown.

What does God demand of us? Successful ministries? Effective evangelism? Expanding churches? No. God demands faithfulness.

Christ's key message to the church in Philadelphia was 'Don't quit.'

Philadelphia was the youngest of the seven cities. It had been set up by Alexander the Great as a means of spreading the Greek culture and way of life to the barbarians. It was a small city and had never really recovered its population following the earthquake in AD 17.

Although it was only thirty miles down the road from Sardis, this church was very different. It was small and struggling. But Christ warmly commended them: 'You are wonderfully faithful. You may be small and lacking strength, but you have kept my word to endure; you haven't denied me.'

Sometimes we think faithful means never changing. It does not. Being faithful to God and to the church sometimes does require change. It also means being obedient, carrying on and not giving up. This is what God loves and commends. That is why he has no criticism for this church, just as he had no criticism for the church in Smyrna.

If you are struggling to stay faithful and feel like giving up, you are in good company. Moses felt like giving up. He was the pastor of 2 million people. Elijah and Jeremiah felt like giving up. Even Paul felt like giving up, in 2 Corinthians. When you feel like giving up and you find yourself just hanging on to God, he can bless you. Because when you are weak, you are strong. This is what Jesus is saying to the church in Philadelphia, and to us: 'You are faithful. I will keep you.'

Perhaps you belong to a small church and are struggling with all the demands of ministry. Perhaps you are the only Christian in your family or workplace and you are feeling the strain of dealing with constant criticism. Let God's faithfulness inspire you and be your example:

Keep your eyes on Jesus, who both began and finished this race we're in. Study how he did it. Because he never lost sight of where he was headed – that exhilarating finish in and with God – he could put up with anything along the way: Cross, shame, whatever. And now he's *there*, in the place of honor, right alongside God. When you find yourselves flagging in your faith, go over that story again, item by item, that long litany of hostility he plowed through. *That* will shoot adrenaline into your souls!

(Hebrews 12:1–3, MSG)

Day 24

Read Revelation 3:7–13
Key verses: Revelation 3:7, 9, 11

....

[7] These are the words of him who is holy and true, who holds the key of David. What he opens no one can shut, and what he shuts no one can open . . .[9] I will make those who are of the synagogue of Satan, who claim to be Jews though they are not, but are liars – I will make them come and fall down at your feet and acknowledge that I have loved you . . . [11] I am coming soon. Hold on to what you have, so that no one will take your crown.

Words of encouragement can have a powerful impact, and when they come from Christ, they are priceless.

Here Christ speaks words of encouragement to this battle-weary church in Philadelphia and to all present-day believers. He urges them not to give up, not to quit, because he is giving them three blessings:

• A present opportunity (verse 7)

In the hands of Jesus is the key of David. He lays before the church a wonderful opportunity. Wherever you are spiritually, wherever you are physically, whatever your trials, troubles or heartbreak, Jesus can offer you a door of opportunity. Even in the midst of your suffering, Jesus can bring you to a place where he can bless and use you. I have found that the experiences my wife and I have wept over together, and the breaking and bruising that the Lord has done in our lives, have provided tremendous opportunities for ministry. I would not be without them. (For more on the subject of suffering and my own experience, read my book, *Invest Your Suffering*, IVP, 2013.)

• A public vindication (verse 9)

Some people assume that the scene in verse 9 refers to the end of time. I suspect that is right, but it may also mean that those who are their worst enemies will become their dearest friends. God will convert these people. He is in the business of converting his enemies and making them his friends. He did it with me and you.

• A permanent reward (verse 11)

This small church was struggling, but it had a glorious future. Jesus will return and they will receive their crown.

Let Christ's words of encouragement nourish your soul.

As you press on in difficult days, keep in mind the public vindication and the permanent reward you will one day receive. Imagine Christ placing the crown on your head and saying, 'Well done, good and faithful servant!' (Matthew 25:21).

Today, in the midst of your hardships, look out for the door of opportunity God is holding open for you. It could be the opportunity to witness to a non-Christian friend, to grieve with someone who is suffering, or to share with other parents who are dealing with similar issues to you.

> Pray for us . . . that God may open a door for our message, so that we may proclaim the mystery of Christ. (Colossians 4:3)

Day 25

Read Revelation 3:14–22
Key verse: Revelation 3:14

....

14 *To the angel of the church in Laodicea write:*

> *These are the words of the Amen, the faithful and true witness, the ruler of God's creation.*

Why do we end our prayers with 'Amen'?

'Amen' simply means 'let it be so', 'this is the truth', 'this is reliable'. So it is hardly surprising that Jesus calls himself the 'Amen'. He is the faithful and true witness. He is completely honest, true and trustworthy. In the Old Testament, God is described as *Elohey Amen*, meaning the true, reliable God (Isaiah 65:16). Psalm 100 encourages us to praise the Lord and come before him with thanksgiving. Why?

> For the LORD is good and his love endures for ever;
>   his faithfulness continues through all generations.
> (verse 5)

The Hebrew word translated 'faithfulness' could be rendered the 'Amen-ness of God'. The psalmist is reminding us that God is reliable. He is the rock and fortress on which we build our lives, the rock on which we stand. He doesn't move or change 'like shifting shadows' (James 1:17).

Christ also introduces himself as 'the ruler of God's creation'. I don't think it is an accident that he introduces himself in such a powerful way to these believers. They had lost sight of whom they were supposed to serve. The Greek word used here for 'ruler' has a wide range of meanings. It can mean origin, beginning, source, author, ruler, governor and master. This verse tells us that Christ existed before the world. Indeed, he is the one who caused the whole world to come into existence (John 1:3). The Bible begins with those great words: 'In the beginning, God created'. Evangelicals have many questions about this topic, but they all agree that God created all things out of nothing, by the power of his Word, for the purpose of his glory.

Jesus made and rules over all things. He holds the universe in place. And yet he came to earth for us. He was nailed to a cross. Such love! Think how much our hearts should beat with love for him.

Are you facing problems today? Come to the solid Rock, which is Christ, and cling to him for strength. He will not let you down. He will not let you go.

My hope is built on nothing less
Than Jesus' blood and righteousness;
I dare not trust the sweetest frame,
But wholly lean on Jesus' name.

On Christ, the solid Rock, I stand;
All other ground is sinking sand,
All other ground is sinking sand.

When darkness veils His lovely face,
I rest on His unchanging grace;
In every high and stormy gale,
My anchor holds within the veil.

His oath, His covenant, His blood
Support me in the whelming flood;
When all around my soul gives way,
He then is all my hope and stay.
(Edward Mote, 1834)

Don't imagine your concerns are too big or complicated for Christ to deal with. He is the God of the universe! He has pinned the stars in the galaxies and he brings the sun up each morning. Nothing is too big for him.

Day 26

Read Revelation 3:14–22
Key verses: Revelation 3:15–16

••

15 I know your deeds, that you are neither cold nor hot. I wish you were either one or the other! 16 So, because you are lukewarm – neither hot nor cold – I am about to spit you out of my mouth.

Imagine the government offering your city money for renovations, and city officials replying, 'No thanks. We're so rich, we don't need your help.' It's unthinkable!

But Laodicea was such an immensely rich and prosperous city that it declined help to rebuild after the earthquake in AD 17. This vibrant commercial centre had it all, except one thing – good water. Situated in the Lycos Valley, it was near to Hierapolis, where there were medicinal hot springs, and Colossae, where there was wonderful, cold, gushing water. But Laodicea's water came from five miles down the road. It contained lime, travelled along a lead pipe and was warmed in the sun, so it tasted of lime, lead and was tepid. No wonder you took a drink and instantly spat it out. Jesus says, 'Actually, that's what your church makes me feel like doing.'

The believers were not refreshing like the icy water from Colossae, or hot like the water in Hierapolis. They were just tepid. This brash, proud church made Jesus sick. It had no power, suffering, sacrifice, emotion or enthusiasm. It was a respectable, nominal, flabby, anaemic, irresolute church. There was no passion for Jesus, for purity, for lost souls or for justice.

It made Jesus sick. Why? Because he never held back anything for us. He went all the way to Calvary. He died there for us. Jesus says to us, 'Whoever wants to be my disciple must deny themselves and take up their cross and follow me' (Matthew 16:24). When he said that, he was going to Calvary. Death is not just something that happens at the end of Christian life when you go through terrible suffering. As a disciple, you have to die daily to self. Christianity is not about self-affirmation; it's about self-denial, about putting Jesus first.

It is easy to say we love Jesus. Talk is cheap. But my prayer is: 'Lord, can I love you more each day? Can I respond to Calvary love more fully? Please God, give me that love in my heart.'

Are you loving God as you should today?

How does God know that you love him? In what ways are you demonstrating your love for God through self-denial and sacrifice? Pray that today you would respond more fully to Christ's Calvary love.

O Love that will not let me go,
I rest my weary soul in thee;
I give thee back the life I owe,
That in thine ocean depths its flow
May richer, fuller be.

O Cross that liftest up my head,
I dare not ask to fly from thee;
I lay in dust life's glory dead,
And from the ground there blossoms red
Life that shall endless be.
(George Matheson, 1882)

Day 27

Read Revelation 3:14–22
Key verses: Revelation 3:17–18

....

> [17] *You say, 'I am rich; I have acquired wealth and do not need a thing.' But you do not realise that you are wretched, pitiful, poor, blind and naked. [18] I counsel you to buy from me gold refined in the fire, so that you can become rich; and white clothes to wear, so that you can cover your shameful nakedness; and salve to put on your eyes, so that you can see.*

Sometimes, instead of being a light, the church mirrors the world.

The citizens of Laodicea boasted of their material prosperity. They were proud of their banks and clothing industry, and their medical school, which was renowned for its Phrygian powder, a paste applied to your eyes to help you see more clearly. These people thought they had it all.

The church mirrored this sickening complacency. Jesus says, 'You're like a wretched beggar and you're not even aware of it. You've got all these wonderful programmes in your church but, spiritually, you're a million miles away from me.' They were sinning and not even aware of it. They had seared their consciences and were no longer able to see what was wrong or how serious their sin was.

In verse 18 Christ refers to the three items that the Laodiceans were particularly proud of. In a warm and compelling way, he says, 'Come to me as you are, and I will give you everything you need. I will give you real treasure. There's nothing wrong with having money in the bank, but I will give you a treasure that lasts for ever – myself. I will give you clean clothes. No more black woollen robes that you manufacture as a status symbol, but white robes! My blood will cleanse you of all sin, and you will be clothed in righteousness. I will give you eye salve to help you see clearly for the very first time.'

People without Christ can have all the things of the world, yet they're blind. They don't know where they have come from or where they are going, and they have no purpose. God promises to open our eyes and show us the truth – that we were made in his image, to know, love and experience him. When we leave this world, is it death? No, it's real life. It's out of the prison and into the palace.

There was no heresy or persecution in this wealthy church. From the outside, it looked comfortable, prosperous and successful. But, in truth, this complacent church was bankrupt. It had lost sight of what real treasure was.

We are so easily duped into believing that having plenty of money, clothes with the right labels, and good health make us rich. Don't become like the believers in Laodicea – complacent in their own good fortune, ignorant of how greatly they had sinned against God and how far from him they had fallen. Christ's arms are outstretched, inviting you into a deeper, growing relationship with him. The question is, will you leave the trinkets of this life and pursue real treasure?

Day 28

Read Revelation 3:14–22
Key verses: Revelation 3:19–20

. . . .

19 Those whom I love I rebuke and discipline. So be earnest and repent. 20 Here I am! I stand at the door and knock. If anyone hears my voice and opens the door, I will come in and eat with that person, and they with me.

Why do we discipline our children? Because we love them and we want them to be the best they can be.

The Lord has said some very harsh things to this church. He's said some very painful things to these Christians. Why? Is it because God is mean? No, it is because he loves them. Sometimes God allows pain in our lives not because he is mean, but because he loves us. He loves us enough to chasten us. God's Word can be incredibly uncomfortable, because he loves us and he wants us to be the best we can be.

And he won't settle. Look at verse 20: 'Here I am! I stand at the door and knock.' This is not an evangelistic text. Jesus is not talking to a non-Christian and saying, 'Let me into your life.' You can apply it that way, I'm sure. But this is primarily a word to the church and to individual Christians. Jesus is saying, 'You have pushed me to the periphery. I want you to put me back in the centre of your life where I used to be.' The results will be radical. When Jesus knocks on the door of your life, he wants to come in and take over. He says, 'This has got to change, this has got to change and this has got to change as well.' We don't like change. That's why we keep the door shut. Jesus is saying to you today, 'Will you let me in? I want to deal with these issues in your life.'

Some Christians want enough of Christ to be identified with him but not enough to be seriously inconvenienced; they genuinely cling to basic Christian orthodoxy but do not want to engage in serious Bible study; they value moral probity, especially of the public sort, but do not engage in war against inner corruptions; they fret over the quality of the preacher's sermon but do not worry much over the quality of their own prayer life. Such Christians are content with mediocrity.
(D. A. Carson, *A Call to Spiritual Reformation*, IVP, 1992, p. 121)

Don't settle for mediocrity! Is Jesus knocking on the door of your life? Is there some area that you have kept compartmentalized, some part you don't want him to touch or change? Swing the door open wide, grant him unlimited access, repent for the sins he points out and, with the Holy Spirit's help, embrace the changes he wants you to make.

Day 29

Read Revelation 3:14–22
Key verses: Revelation 3:21–22

···

> ²¹ *To the one who is victorious, I will give the right to sit with me on my throne, just as I was victorious and sat down with my Father on his throne.* ²² *Whoever has ears, let them hear what the Spirit says to the churches.*

Did you notice that in all these letters there is a little phrase at the end: 'the one who is victorious'. It could be translated as 'the one who conquers' (ESV) or 'the one who overcomes' (NKJV).

Who are these 'overcomers'? We might imagine them to be spiritual giants, such as missionaries, pastors and church leaders – those inspirational Christians whom we typically put on a pedestal. But 'overcomers' are not an elite category of Christians who live triumphant lives and don't seem to have any problems. No! Being an 'overcomer' means that you persevere. You keep going and don't give up. Guess what? I have a million problems and so have you. You struggle in your home, in your marriage, with your kids, with work and witnessing for Christ. Sometimes you feel terrible and you let Christ down. But if you persevere – and Christ gives you the grace to persevere – you're an 'overcomer'.

This perseverance isn't a passive stance. Over and over again, in every one of the letters we are urged to 'hear what the Spirit says to the churches' (verse 22). If we are going to be 'overcomers', we need to listen to God's Word and obey it, letting it do its work of transformation in our lives. As James taught,

> Do not merely listen to the word, and so deceive your-selves. Do what it says. Anyone who listens to the word but does not do what it says is like someone who looks at his face in a mirror and, after looking at himself, goes away and immediately forgets what he looks like. But whoever looks intently into the perfect law that gives freedom, and continues in it – not forgetting what they have heard but doing it – they will be blessed in what they do.
> (James 1:22–25)

There is no elite category of Christian who has a hotline to God and enjoys extra spiritual insights and favour. You can be victorious. You can be an overcomer. There is no deep secret or quick fix to achieving this enduring spiritual life. It is a lifetime commitment consisting of daily decisions to follow God – putting him first, spending time in his Word, obeying him through the power of his Holy Spirit. You may have been on this journey of faith many years, you may be just starting out, or you may have recently come back to God. Christ's word to you is the same: keep persevering.

> Blessed is the one who perseveres under trial because, having stood the test, that person will receive the crown of life that the Lord has promised to those who love him.
>
> (James 1:12)

> May the Lord direct your hearts into God's love and Christ's perseverance.
>
> (2 Thessalonians 3:5)

Day 30

Read Revelation 3:14–22
Key verse: Revelation 3:21

....

²¹ To the one who is victorious, I will give the right to sit with me on my throne, just as I was victorious and sat down with my Father on his throne.

A seven-year-old boy was asked, 'What is home?' He thought for a minute and then replied, 'Home is a place that when you get to it, they've got to let you in.'

Because of what Christ achieved for us on the cross, heaven is our home. Did you notice that at the end of every one of the letters there is a promise of heaven? To the believers in Laodicea the promise was, you will 'sit with me on my throne'. Christ's last word to each of these struggling Christians is: 'You'll be home soon.'

Our great hope of heaven is that we will see Jesus:

He's the apostle of our faith. He's the anointed one. The atoning sacrifice. He's the author of our salvation. He is the altogether lovely one. He is the beautiful Saviour. The bread of heaven. The bridegroom of our souls. He's the bright morning star. He is the chief shepherd and the capstone. He's the captain of the armies of the Lord. He is the conqueror of death.

He is the Christ. He is fully God and fully man, full of grace and truth. He is the fairest of 10,000. He is the faithful one. He is the friend of sinners. He is the glorious Redeemer, the gate for the sheep, the good shepherd. He is great David's greatest Son. He is the Holy One. He is the head of the church, the high priest, after the order of Melchizedek.

He is the image of the invisible God. He is Immanuel, God is with us. He is the joy of his people and the justifier of the ungodly. He is the King of Israel, King of the Jews and King of kings. He is my kinsman-redeemer, the light of the world, the lion of Judah, the lamb of Calvary. He is the meek and majestic one. He is the mighty God, the everlasting Father, the Prince of peace. He is the man of sorrows, acquainted with grief.

He is the Passover Lamb. He is the root of David, the rock of ages, the risen and ascended Lord. He is my Redeemer. He is the sinless one. He is the true vine and the tender shoot. He is the true light of true light. He is the wisdom of God. He is the Word of God. He is the way, the truth and the life. He is my Saviour. He is mine.

Heaven is about Jesus. The greatest joy of our hearts is that we'll be able to see him for ever. Prepare for heaven now – serve him with all your heart and live for his glory.

Today, meditate on Revelation 22:1–5. Ultimately, our home will be the new heavens and the new earth. Live your life with this destination in mind, daily investing in eternity.

For further study

If you would like to do further study on Revelation, the following books may be useful:

- Craig Keener, *Revelation*, NIV Application Commentary (Zondervan, 2000)

- Leon Morris, *Revelation*, Tyndale New Testament Commentary (IVP, 2009)

- John Stott, *What Christ Thinks of the Church* (Monarch, 2003)

- Michael Wilcock, *The Message of Revelation*, The Bible Speaks Today (IVP, 1991)

- Tom Wright, *Revelation for Everyone* (SPCK, 2014)

KESWICK MINISTRIES

Our purpose

Keswick Ministries is committed to the spiritual renewal of God's people for his mission in the world.

God's purpose is to bring his blessing to all the nations of the world. That promise of blessing, which touches every aspect of human life, is ultimately fulfilled through the life, death, resurrection, ascension and future return of Christ. All of the people of God are called to participate in his missionary purposes, wherever he may place them. The central vision of Keswick Ministries is to see the people of God equipped, encouraged and refreshed to fulfil that calling, directed and guided by God's Word in the power of his Spirit, for the glory of his Son.

Our priorities

Keswick Ministries seeks to serve the local church through:

• *Hearing God's Word*: the Scriptures are the foundation for the church's life, growth and mission, and Keswick Ministries is committed to preaching and teaching God's Word in a way that is faithful to Scripture and relevant to Christians of all ages and backgrounds.

- *Becoming like God's Son*: from its earliest days the Keswick movement has encouraged Christians to live godly lives in the power of the Spirit, to grow in Christ-likeness and to live under his lordship in every area of life. This is God's will for his people in every culture and generation.

- *Serving God's mission*: the authentic response to God's Word is obedience to his mission, and the inevitable result of Christlikeness is sacrificial service. Keswick Ministries seeks to encourage committed discipleship in family life, work and society, and energetic engagement in the cause of world mission.

Our ministry

- *Keswick: the event.* Every summer the town of Keswick hosts a three-week convention, which attracts some 15,000 Christians from the UK and around the world. The event provides Bible teaching for all ages, vibrant worship, a sense of unity across generations and denominations, and an inspirational call to serve Christ in the world. It caters for children of all ages and has a strong youth and young adult programme. And it all takes place in the beautiful Lake District – a perfect setting for rest, recreation and refreshment.

- *Keswick: the movement.* For 140 years the work of Keswick has had an impact on churches worldwide, and today the movement is underway throughout the UK, as well as in many parts of Europe, Asia, North America, Australia, Africa and the Caribbean. Keswick Ministries is committed to strengthening the network in the UK and beyond, through prayer, news, pioneering and cooperative activity.

- *Keswick resources.* Keswick Ministries produces a range of books and booklets based on the core foundations of Christian life and mission. It makes Bible teaching available through free access to mp3 downloads, and the sale of DVDs and CDs. It broadcasts online through Clayton TV and annual BBC Radio 4 services.

- *Keswick teaching and training.* In addition to the summer convention, Keswick Ministries is developing teaching and training events that will happen at other times of the year and in other places.

Our unity

The Keswick movement worldwide has adopted a key Pauline statement to describe its gospel inclusivity: 'for you are all one in Christ Jesus' (Galatians 3:28). Keswick Ministries works with evangelicals from a wide variety of church backgrounds, on the understanding that they share a commitment to the essential truths of the Christian faith as set out in its statement of belief.

Our contact details
T: 01768 780075
E: info@keswickministries.org
W: www.keswickministries.org
Mail: Keswick Ministries, Rawnsley Centre, Main Street, Keswick, Cumbria CA12 5NP, England

Related titles from IVP

Food for the Journey

The Food for the Journey series offers daily devotionals from well-loved Bible teachers at the Keswick Convention in an ideal pocket-sized format – to accompany you wherever you go.

Available in the series

1 Thessalonians
Alec Motyer with
Elizabeth McQuoid
978 1 78359 439 9

Habakkuk
Jonathan Lamb with
Elizabeth McQuoid
978 1 78359 652 2

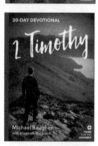

2 Timothy
Michael Baughen with
Elizabeth McQuoid
978 1 78359 438 2

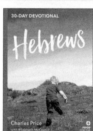

Hebrews
Charles Price with
Elizabeth McQuoid
978 1 78359 611 9

Ezekiel
Liam Goligher with
Elizabeth McQuoid
978 1 78359 603 4

James
Stuart Briscoe with
Elizabeth McQuoid
978 1 78359 523 5

Available from your local Christian bookshop or **www.ivpbooks.com**

Food for the Journey

John 14 - 17
Simon Manchester with
Elizabeth McQuoid
978 1 78359 495 5

Ruth
Alistair Begg with
Elizabeth McQuoid
978 1 78359 525 9

Revelation
Paul Mallard with
Elizabeth McQuoid
978 1 78359 712 3

Praise for the series

'This devotional series is biblically rich, theologically deep and full of wisdom . . . I recommend it highly.' **Becky Manley Pippert, speaker, author of** *Out of the Saltshaker and into the World* **and creator of the Live/Grow/Know course and series of books**

'These devotional guides are excellent tools.' **John Risbridger, Minister and Team Leader, Above Bar Church, Southampton**

'These bite-sized banquets . . . reveal our loving Father weaving the loose and messy ends of our everyday lives into his beautiful, eternal purposes in Christ.' **Derek Burnside, Principal, Capernwray Bible School**

'I would highly recommend this series of 30-day devotional books to anyone seeking a tool that will help [him or her] to gain a greater love of scripture, or just simply . . . to do something out of devotion. Whatever your motivation, these little books are a must-read.' **Claud Jackson,** *Youthwork* **Magazine**

Available from your local Christian bookshop or **www.ivpbooks.com**

Related teaching CD and DVD packs

CD PACKS

1 Thessalonians
SWP2203D (5-CD pack)

2 Timothy
SWP2202D (4-CD pack)

Ezekiel
SWP2263D (5-CD pack)

Habakkuk
SWP2299D (5-CD pack)

Hebrews
SWP2281D (5-CD pack)

James
SWP2239D (4-CD pack)

John 14 - 17
SWP2238D (5-CD pack)

Revelation
SWP2300D (5-CD pack)

Ruth
SWP2280D (5-CD pack)

DVD PACKS

Ezekiel
SWP2263A (5-DVD pack)

Habakkuk
SWP2299A (5-DVD pack)

John 14 - 17
SWP2238A (5-DVD pack)

Revelation
SWP2300A (5-DVD pack)

Ruth
SWP2280A (5-DVD pack)